NOURISH

"Let all of God's children feed off of the environment"

By Kenya McGhee
Illustrated by Donna Brown

AuthorHouse™
1663 Liberty Drive
Bloomington, IN 47403
www.authorhouse.com
Phone: 833-262-8899

Because of the dynamic nature of the Internet, any web addresses or links contained in this book may have changed
since publication and may no longer be valid. The views expressed in this work are solely those of the author and do
not necessarily reflect the views of the publisher, and the publisher hereby disclaims any responsibility for them.

Any people depicted in stock imagery provided by Getty Images are models,
and such images are being used for illustrative purposes only.
Certain stock imagery © Getty Images.

This book is printed on acid-free paper.

ISBN: 979-8-8230-2530-0 (sc)
979-8-8230-2531-7 (e)

Library of Congress Control Number: 2024908078

Print information available on the last page.

Published by AuthorHouse 04/25/2024

authorHOUSE®

This Faith-based book is a brief motivational affirmation story depicting only a few contributing facts that help support a child's healthy development throughout their stages in life.

A very intimate creation of the author's personal story and gorgeously collaborated illustrations from Donna Brown.

Introduction to an "Innocent Seed"

Term: An Innocent seed is any child birthed into the bad soil of any suffocating surrounding affliction of various ill-advised influences which initially arrest their development at conception. They suffer throughout a significant portion of their shape & molding, informative processing years of life, deprived of proper nourishment they consume numerous toxins daily that confuse, stick and weigh down a soul misdirecting a healthy course which normally impedes development mentally and physically, and without the proper tools or assisting outlets life will usually lead them down a tumultuous whirlwind journey of damaging corrupted paths attaching strongholds, detours away from making healthy decisions that facilitate steps towards successful living.

Let all of God's children feed off of the environment
Allow the first love of grace to be heartfelt inside the miraculous wonder of a
fearfully & wonderfully planted creation growing inside a mother's womb

Jeremiah 29:11

For I know the plans I have for you, says the Lord.
They are plans for good and not for disaster, to give you a future and hope

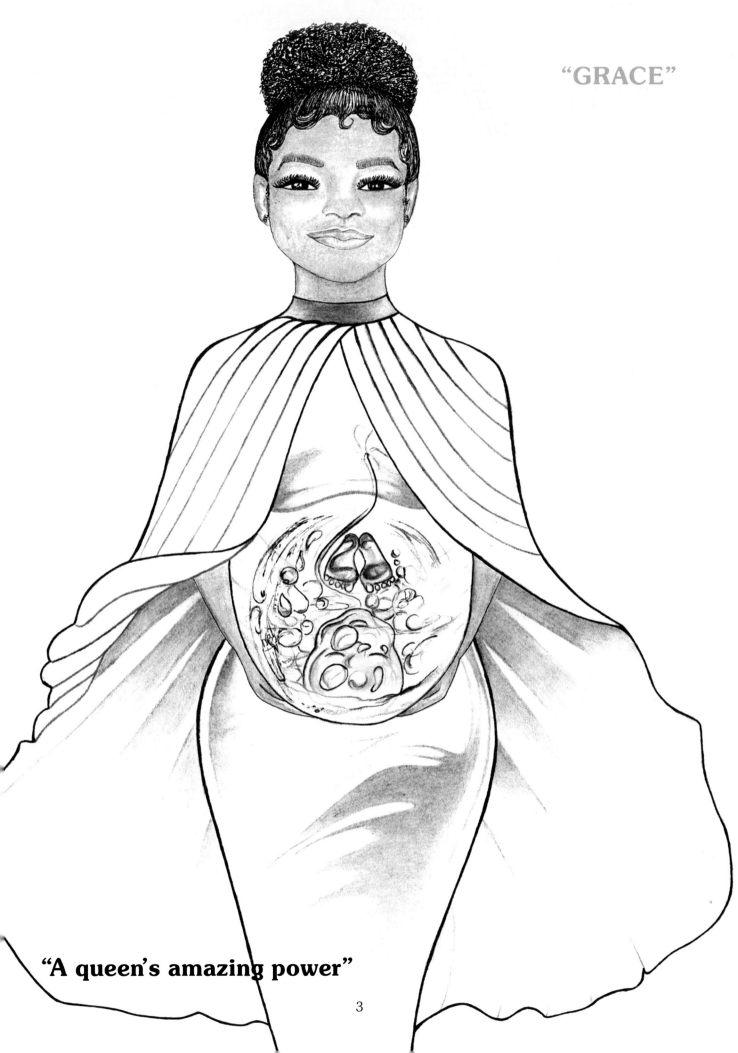

"GRACE"

"A queen's amazing power"

3

Let a family unit's hands feed and nurture a child with overwhelming embracement providing hope and a greater outlook on life

"FORCEFUL BONDING LOVE"

Take time out to share family moments
Create invaluable embedded memories that will forevermore stimulate a child's mind helping them to grow & hold onto traditional healthy family functions

Let's cherish and be grateful for our amazing birthed blessing
Innocent Seeds the kisses of life sent from up above.

"Our Most High"

Bonding Love...

motherly

Throughout *every* stage of development let's attentively support our Innocent Seeds strengthening their lives by an atmosphere of holistic nourishment

Let's feed our children with fruits grown in the good soil of this land then overtime their lives will surely expand

Assuring them a wholesome development so then independently they can securely take their very own first stand, reflecting an irremovable robust stance

fatherly

Children be lifelong students in this world as the ages of life pass you by

Face your fears, continue to positively live, learn & grow

Good and bad social experiences created by every friendship will build values in character instilling powerful tools from each unique encounter along your traveled roads

In confidence walk with highly esteemed strides and build your standards on the nourishing ingredients inside the lessons of your teaching throughout every stage of life

Self-Love

A,a B,b C,c

ABBA

Learn / Grow / Bond

Lead

LIVE LOVE

B E K I N D

INVEST IN YOURSELF

The forever changing climate of rainy situations will dampen some- days therefore expect things to happen & understand that all life stages will have its painful struggles and sadness, and life won't always feel great.

However, the storms of this world don't last always remember that God's grace and mercy is renewed each day so hold onto Faith.

There is beauty in new beginning look for that infinite sun that continuously shine it overrides any darkness and wipe away any storm.

Change your views by keeping an open-mind.
Renew your mind and eliminate distractions by letting go of things that need to be left behind.

Understand that you hold the ability to weather any storm so try to avoid emotional stress & allow tomorrow's elevation of a new day to lift you above harm.

"Be Encouraged"

And when the sun is up the rays are warm and consoling to an influential upbringing.

As a child exits their loving comfort zone entering society alone the nourishing tools from their shape and molding will successfully navigate them through their journey along with a compassionate community filled with neighbors whom so kindly embrace and assist the next generation's pure Innocent Seeds to flourish by extending their helping hands because.

"It takes a village to raise an Innocent Seed"

neighborly

ROLE MODELS EMPOWER

Rooted and secure in love lets value and nourish our next generation's future of this world in all areas of life.

Allow them to feed off of the environment that surround them our children are birthed into this earth's soil with utter pureness "Innocent Seeds".

Let's water them daily so they can flourish in worth, esteem, identity and wisdom, shape and molding them with nothingness than illuminating light that positively influence.

Raise forceful barriers that protect them along this world's journey.

"It takes a village to raise an Innocent Seed"

LOVE/ PEACE /UNITY

to all mankind

sewing seeds of greatness

Behold expose our Innocent Seeds to the divine power of a sacred church home setting the children on top of a vital, solid foundation.

Permit the living word of God to be internalized & permeate souls.

Let's build our children to be believers who trust in the Lord and live lives inclined towards Faith.

So when a child get lost and roams astray the almighty Savior will illuminate the pavement, stabilizing shaky roads and direct a better way along their growth's journey.

Allow salvation to prepare their minds and hearts, the ultimate resource for everything in life.

So when the pressure of this world feel like it's too much to bear they'll know that God will provide strength, wisdom, understanding and energy to carry them through.

"Anticipate higher levels of increase"

"Prepare their minds and hearts"

Start children off on the way they should go,
and even when they are old they will not turn from it
- Proverbs 22:6

Making visits to local museums can be informative experiences to gain knowledge of our culture's creativity & historical hidden past.

Observe extinct figures, painting and sculptures by touring the exhibit of one's artistry.

Live to dream as a visionary, create, imagine and aspire to plant your very own lasting seeds of nourishment in this world.

Enlighten our children by pulling up ancestral roots, fundamentals of our history past miles.

Activate visions and dreams so they too can create greater things. Help them visualize and understand the actions and sweat from powerful groundbreaking leaders, the voices, hands and movements that will eternally touch humanity, legacies that continue to breathe beyond measure.

Kamala Harris our very first female African American/Asian 49th Vice President in America's history who stands in the shadow of a way maker.

Shirley A. Chisholm the very first black woman to be elected in the United States Congress serving seven terms she was the first black candidate for a major party nomination.

Frederick Douglass a social reformist, abolitionist, orator and writer and most important a prominent leader of the African American civil rights movement during the 19th century.

Booker T. Washington an American educator, curator and author between 1890-1915

21

Children decisions are your destiny.

There is only one truth, one way continue to be guided by light.

Elevate and strive to reach incredible heights.

Your days will become more confusing and complex, but also clearer as adulthood quicken.

Every minute time elapse, life will be filled with decisions to make, the adversary will attack and negative temptations of this world's deception will approach you, attempting to steer you wrong. With the proper nourishment your skilled, standing fully equip strong.

Anchored in righteousness, shielded by the light you will bypass the corruption of strongholds. With the instilled knowledge & power to choose the right roads.

Understand & recognize the supernatural power held within

"ENDURE"

"STAND"

"BELIEVE"

"INSIDE DETERMINATION BE DIFFERENT"

"RESILIENTLY PERSEVERE"

"PERSISTENTLY CHALLENGE"

"CLIMB"

"ACHIEVE"

OVERCOMING THE ODDS

"ASCEND INTO AUTHENTICITY"

IDENTITY

"LIFE TREASURED DISCOVERY"

grow comfortable conquering difficult challenges
and gradually progress

Children grace will always carry you through unveiling character and strength to pass any test. The human error of bad choices, mistakes and failure will occur along your journey allow consequences to be lessons learned.

Dig deep to rise above insecurities resiliently adapt, adjust and stand flexibility is key.

Surpass all perceived limits by discovering your abundance in the river that everlastingly flows. There's a gift of supernatural power that you hold within tap into it to triumph over any obstacle as you continue your lifelong process of development "Keep Growing in Confidence & Courage".

"Life is full of decisions, error, and process
it's up to you to patiently endure
and properly choose your destiny"
K. Mcghee

"Recognize Gods first endless love"

Recognizing Gods first love for me enables me to see touch and walk towards the unseen "FAITH".

Uplifting, I receive so much joy as my thirst continue to drink from the infinite river that everlastingly flow in abundance.

Right before my eyes everything shift as the living word manifest inside my soul then I truly recognize Gods first love.

It takes me by utter surprise accelerating my emotions it elevate me to indescribable incredible heights.

It instills the super to my natural and when the spirit encounter a spirit the sensation is why I cry elation tears of gratitude.

And I'm favored daily consuming his warm eternal sun rays day after day by & by.

It's moving me beyond the depths of sin.

It's bringing fruition to my reset life goals and dreams.

It replenishes my body when perspired sweat from every hopeful labored action is put forth.

Even when the ages of life don't appear as they should it just take the simple choice for me to trust & believe.

Recognizing Gods first love for me.

And in that very moment restraints are released and I can live life freely knowing that I was too chosen and loved unconditionally & that's more grand than any mother thing.

So can how can I live deficient

McGhee, Kenya

"Fallen Wings"

Symptoms: despair, defeat, hopelessness, no fresh air to breathe, lifeless, weak, utter darkness, giving up, silent no words to speak

Every time we fall understand that we carry the cure, the ability to rise.
It's okay to release emotions unload confined tears that anchor the soul cry.
Awaken insight rising with a sharper perspective through opened eyes.
Trust & believe that during grim times throughout our loneliest valley an Almighty Savior is hovering he rides.
Throughout every affliction, bad choice and failure, every denial and rejection in every aspect of our lives it's still up.
We must endure highly motivated stepping with enhanced strides gifted rejuvenated lifted.
Restoration builds muscle and repairs damaged wings so we can fly again.
No matter your circumstance inside perseverance liken to a cat with 9 lives refacing demise be wise and refuse to die.
Never accept living inactive at the bottom wasting your gift of invaluable time rise.
Again & again even when the normal emotions of desperation occur.

With a tight grip on Faith continue a robust stance standing maintaining your reach.
Regroup inside self-discovery by renewing your mind.
Transforming your actions and speech walk into yourself gradually overtime laying to rest your decaying past.

Because every time we fall understand that we develop and carry the cure, the ability to rise.
Educated through our experiences we are provided a sharper perspective through opened eyes
Fallen Wings.

McGhee, Kenya
2024

About the Author

Kenya L. McGhee currently a reformed incarcerated inmate born September of 1974 out of Toledo, Ohio whom has transformed her testimonial recovery from her upbringing back-story trials into survival, empowerment and inspiration. Serving a fifteen year prison term Kenya was birthed into a home with an open door to street-life, the opposite of what this brief story depicts.

Never thinking or knowing the painful backlash of damaging chain reaction aftereffects due to her crime Kenya and her co-defendant her very own father co-conspired in a crime that led to his demise and also another.

Recovering from the typical street-life behaviors of crime, addiction and utter corrupting dysfunction Kenya's passionate mission today is to give back to the community by depositing her light of nourishment. Kenya's hopes are to open the eyes and touch Innocent seeds with relatable journeys as well as to redirect troubled paths of self-sabotaging afflictions that ultimately lead to incarceration or any other dark pits in life.

Printed in the United States
by Baker & Taylor Publisher Services